CROCHET PATTERNS FOR CHRISTMAS

Amigurumi Crochet Santa, Snowman and Christmas Ornaments & Tree Decorations

Content

Introduction

Welcome to "Crochet Patterns for Christmas," a comprehensive collection of crochet patterns designed to bring joy and creativity to your holiday season. In this book, we have curated a wide range of patterns that will help you create beautiful and festive decorations, gifts, and accessories using the art of crochet.

The holiday season is a time of warmth, love, and cherished traditions. What better way to celebrate than by adding a personal touch to your decorations and gifts? With the help of this book, you will be able to infuse your home and presents with the charm and uniqueness that only handmade crochet items can bring.

Whether you are an experienced crocheter or just starting out, "Crochet Patterns for Christmas" offers something for everyone. From adorable ornaments and stockings to cozy blankets and hats, you will find patterns that suit various skill levels and preferences. Each pattern is accompanied by clear instructions, detailed stitch diagrams, and helpful tips to ensure your crochet journey is enjoyable and successful.

Not only will you be able to create stunning pieces for your own home, but you will also have the opportunity to spread holiday cheer by gifting your handmade creations to loved ones. Handcrafted items hold a special place in the hearts of recipients, as they are a testament to the time, effort, and thoughtfulness put into each stitch.

We hope that "Crochet Patterns for Christmas" inspires you to embark on a delightful crochet adventure and adds an extra touch of magic to your holiday season. May these patterns bring you joy, relaxation, and a sense of accomplishment as you create beautiful crochet masterpieces that will be treasured for years to come.

Happy crocheting and Merry Christmas!

Crochet Basics

Supplies & Tools For Crocheting

You will need a few tools on hand to be able to crochet a bag apart from yarn. When you use the correct tools, it makes crocheting a bag easy and enjoyable. Below, we'll focus on some of the best tools you'll want to have to be able to make a stunning bag.

Crochet Hooks

A crochet hook is a must-have tool for making bags. They are used to create the stitches that form the bags, and the type of hook you use can affect the size, tension, and overall appearance of your projects. There are different types of crochet hooks available, including traditional hooks and ergonomic hooks. **Traditional hooks** have a tapered shaft and a hook on one end. They are typically made of aluminum, steel, or plastic and come in a variety of sizes. Traditional hooks are suitable for most crocheting projects and are widely available in craft stores and online.

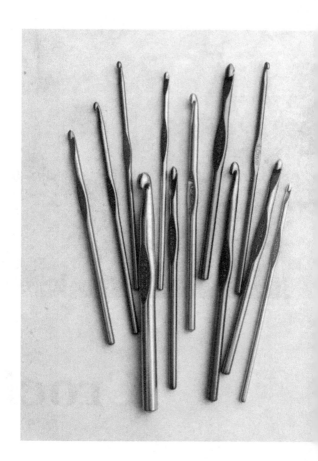

Ergonomic hooks, on the other hand, have a more ergonomic design that reduces hand fatigue and strain. They have a thicker handle or grip that makes them more comfortable to hold for extended periods. Ergonomic hooks are available in various materials, such as rubber, bamboo, and plastic, and are becoming increasingly popular among crocheters. These are my favorite crochet hooks to use when making bags.

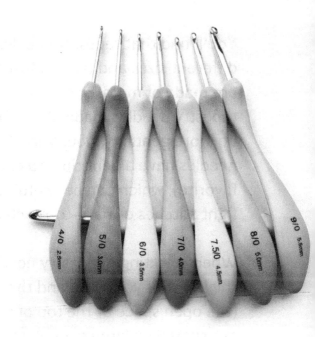

When selecting a crochet hook, consider the type of yarn you're using and the tension you want to achieve. Generally, thicker yarn requires a larger hook, while thinner yarn requires a smaller hook, but check the yarn label to be sure. Most crochet hook sets will include a range of sizes, allowing you to experiment and find the perfect hook size for your project.

Tapestry Needles

Tapestry needles are an essential tool for finishing your projects. These blunt-tipped needles are used for weaving in the loose ends of yarn and sewing the projects together to create a larger project. Without a tapestry needle, your project may appear unfinished or may unravel over time.

You'll find that tapestry needles come in different sizes and types. Most tapestry needles are made of metal or plastic, but there are also tapestry needles made of bamboo, which can be more gentle on your yarn. Some tapestry needles have a bent tip or a curved shape (my favorite), which can be useful for working on tight stitches or hard-to-reach areas.

When selecting a tapestry needle, consider the thickness of your yarn and the size of the eye (the open space at the top of the needle). The eye should be large enough to accommodate the yarn, but not so large that it slips out while you're weaving in the ends. You may also want to consider the type of material the needle is made of, as some materials may be more gentle on your yarn than others.

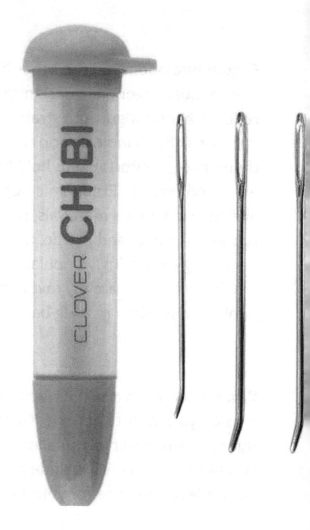

To use a tapestry needle, thread the loose end of your yarn through the eye of the needle and weave it in and out of the stitches on the back side of your bag. Once the end is woven in, trim the excess yarn. To sew your project together, use a tapestry needle and yarn to join the bags by joining them together at the edges.

Stitch Markers

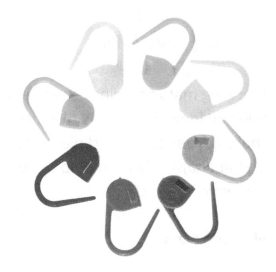

Stitch markers are useful tools for keeping track of your stitches and ensuring that your bag project turns out the way you want it. These markers are small, usually plastic or metal rings, that can be placed on your crochet hook or in your work to mark a specific st or row.

Stitch markers come in different types and sizes, such as locking stitch markers, split-ring stitch markers, and coil-less safety pins. Locking stitch markers are especially useful as they can be opened and closed, allowing you to move them around your work without having to remove them. Split-ring stitch markers and coil-less safety pins are great for marking specific stitches or sections of your work.

When using stitch markers, it's important to place them correctly. They should be placed on the loop of the stitch, not on the post or the hook. If you're working in the round, place a stitch marker at the beginning of your round to mark the start. You can also use stitch markers to indicate increases or decreases, or to mark sections of your pattern that require special attention.
beginning
Stitch markers are especially useful for complex bag patterns, as they can help you keep track of your progress and prevent mistakes. By using stitch markers, you can ensure that your bag project turns out exactly as you want it.

Blocking Mats & Pins

Blocking mats and pins are essential tools for giving your projects a polished, finished look. So, what is blocking exactly? Blocking is the process of stretching and shaping your crocheted pieces to their proper dimensions and allowing them to dry in that shape. This can help to even out sts, straighten edges, and create a more professional finish.

Blocking Mats

Blocking mats are foam mats that can be used to stretch your projects to the desired size and shape. They come in different sizes and thicknesses, so you can choose the one that suits your project. Some blocking mats have a grid printed on them, which can help you to accurately measure and place your projects.

Blocking Pins

Blocking pins are used to hold your projects in place on the blocking mat. These pins are usually rust-proof and come in different lengths and thicknesses. They can be used to pin your projects to the blocking mat, stretching them to the correct size and shape. Blocking pins can also be used to pin together multiple projects, creating a larger project.

Scissors

Scissors are an often-overlooked but essential tool for crocheting projects. While any pair of scissors can technically be used, having a good quality pair can make all the difference in your project.

Sharp scissors are crucial for cutting your yarn cleanly, preventing fraying and splitting. Choose scissors with comfortable handles, as crocheting can be a repetitive motion that can cause hand strain over time. Many crocheters prefer scissors with ergonomic handles or padded grips to reduce hand fatigue.

Another factor to consider when choosing scissors for crocheting is the blade length. Long blades can make it easier to cut multiple strands of yarn at once, while short blades are better for more precise cuts.

When using your scissors, you should only use them for cutting yarn and not for anything else. I call these yarn scissors, and they are ONLY used for yarn at all times. This can help to prevent dulling or damage to the blades. It's also important to keep your scissors clean and sharp, as dull scissors can cause jagged cuts and make it more difficult to work with your yarn.

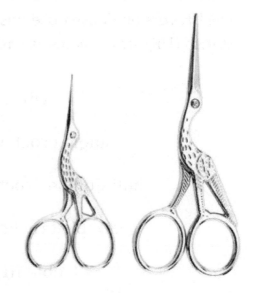

Crochet Instructions

When you're first learning how to crochet, reading written crochet patterns can seem like reading a foreign language. But once you understand the lingo, you'll be stitching away in no time. All you need to know to get started are a few basic stitch abbreviations as well as some common crochet terms.

Learning the Crochet Language

The first thing you need to do to read a written crochet pattern is to become familiar with common crochet terms. Once you understand these terms, you'll use them over and over.

Term Conversions

The two sets are the American English (US) or British English (UK) crochet terms. Every crochet pattern should follow one of these two terminology sets. Converting patterns from US to UK (or vice versa) is easy. The main difference between the two is the most basic of stitches. The US's starting point is the single crochet. However, the UK version doesn't use this term, and calls it a double crochet instead. The British (UK) stitch ladder is basically offset by one from the US terms.

US	UK
single crochet (sc)	double crochet (dc)
half double crochet (hdc)	half treble (htr)
double crochet (dc)	treble (tr)
treble (tr)	double treble (dtr)

Basic Stitch Abbreviations

Here are the abbreviations for the most common crochet stitches you'll encounter in crochet patterns in this book.

ch-chain

sl st-slip st

sc-single crochet

dc– double crochet

tr– Treble Crochet

cl– cluster (explained below)

YO– yarn over

sp-space

WS-Wrong Side of Sweater

RS- Right Side of Sweater

Hdc– half double crochet

HDC2TOG – Half Double Crochet 2 Together

FLO– Crochet into front loops only

BLO– back loop only

MR-magic ring

Inc– increase

Dec– decrease

*6– number of repeats

(12)– total number of stitches in a round

General Techniques

Slip Knot

A slip knot is a type of knot that you'll use to attach the yarn to the crochet hook. Making a slip knot is the first step in many crochet projects. It is made by tying a simple loop at the end of the yarn, then placing the loop on the crochet hook and pulling it tight.

There are various ways to make a slip knot, and everyone has their favorite method.

Here's the first way:

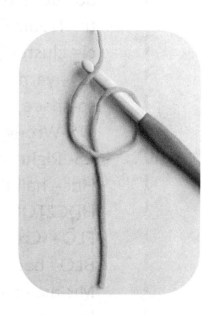

- Pull a length of yarn from the yarn ball.
We'll try to make our slip knot approximately 6 inches away from the tail end of the yarn. This will give us a long enough yarn tail to weave in later.
- Make a loop, crossing the ball yarn over and on top of the tail end.
- Insert the crochet hook into the center of the loop, from front to back. Use the crochet hook to grab the ball-end yarn, and pull it through the center of the loop.

- Pull both ends of the yarn to tighten the loop around the hook. The loop on the crochet hook should be tight, but still loose enough to slide up and down the hook. Make sure that you still have a 6-inch yarn tail that you can weave in later.

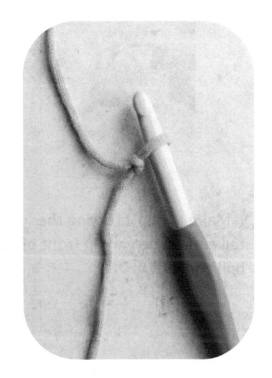

The slip knot is complete, and you are ready to **start crocheting**. To start making ch sts, pinch the base of the slip knot between the thumb and middle finger of your left hand.
Then, start your chain.

Here's another way:

In this method, we'll hold the yarn up in the air, and make the slip knot with just our fingers.

Pull a length of yarn from the yarn ball. Hold the ball end of yarn in your left hand and the tail end of the yarn in your right hand. Make sure to leave at least a 6-inch yarn tail so that you have enough to weave in later.

1. Make a loop, crossing the tail end of the yarn in front of the ball end.

2. With your left hand, pinch the yarn where it overlaps. With your right hand, move the tail end of the yarn behind the open loop.

3. Insert your right-hand fingers through the loop, pinch the tail end of the yarn, and pull it through the loop.

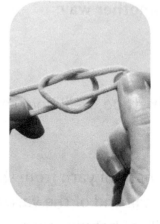

4. With your left hand, pull on the ball end of the yarn to tighten. Slip the knot onto the crochet needle, and pull on the tail end of the yarn to tighten it further.

14

5. The slip knot is complete, and you are ready to start crocheting. Just as before, pinch the base of the slip knot between the thumb and middle finger of your left hand to start making ch sts.

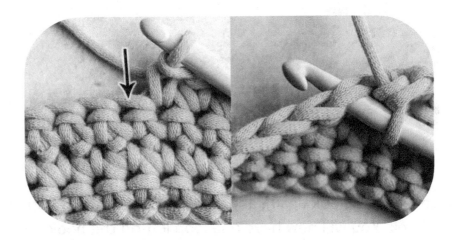

Single Crochet (sc)

The single crochet st is a simple st that's well suited to a wide variety of crochet projects, like pillows, top-down beanies, and warm sweaters. It's often used in doll and amigurumi patterns, too.

The following in an in-depth description of how to make a single crochet st.

1. Insert the hook into the next st. Put the tip of the hook under both of the loops at the top of the st.

2. Bring the yarn over the hook, from back to front, and pull a loop of yarn through the st. You will now have two loops on the hook.

3. Bring the yarn over the hook again, and pull the yarn through both loops on the hook. You will now have one loop left on the hook.

Great job! You have now completed a single crochet (SC) st.

Single Crochet into a Foundation Chain

Often, you'll start a project with ch sts and a row of single crochet. Here's how to do that:

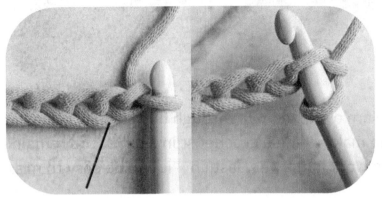

1. Make a slip knot and a foundation ch of 15 sts.
2. To make the first single crochet, insert the hook into the second ch from the hook. (Remember, we don't count the ch that is around the hook.)

3. Yarn over, and pull up a loop

4. Yarn over, and pull through both loops on the hook.

5. Rep Steps 2-4 to make a single crochet st in each of the remaining 14 chs. Be sure to work in the very last ch – it can be easy to miss.

Single Crochet into another Row

After the first row of single crochet, you can turn your work and start another row. To do this, you'll work into the sts of the previous row.

1. Ch 1 and turn your work clockwise. (Keep your hook in the ch st as you turn the work, so you don't lose your place.) You will now be looking at the backside of the previous row.

2. Make a single crochet st in the first st.

3. Continue across the row, making sure to work into the last st.

4. To start another row, ch-1 and turn.

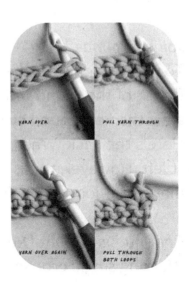

Fastening Off: Cut the yarn, leaving a 6-inch yarn tail. Lift the hook straight up, bringing the yarn tail through the remaining loop on the hook. Pull the yarn tail to tighten the last st. Weave in the yarn ends with a tapestry needle.

Single Crochet in the Round

You can work single crochet in rows or rounds. As you may already know, there are two ways to work in the round: joined rounds and continuous (aka spiral) rounds. In either case, working single crochet in the round is very similar to working single crochet in rows.

SPIRAL   JOINED

Joined Rounds

To work a single crochet in joined rounds, you'll join the last st of the round to the first st of the round with a sl sts. You'll then ch-1, which does not count as a st. Then, start the next round by making a single crochet in the same st as the slip-st join. Here's the trick: When you get to the end of the round, it may look like you have one st left. However, this is not a real st – it is the sl sts join. sk this sl sts and the ch-1, and make your join to the first SC of the round.

Continuous or Spiral Rounds

Working single crochet in spiral rounds is very simple, too. To make continuous rounds:

st around the circle in a spiral pattern.

Make the first st of each round into the first st of the previous round.

Don't join the beg and end of each round with a sl sts. Don't ch up to the next round.

Tip: With continuous rounds, it's a good idea to use a stitch marker to mark the beg of each round, since there won't be a seam!

Half Double Crochet st (HDC)

The half double crochet st is taller than a single crochet st, yet shorter than double crochet st. The process of making a half double crochet st is very similar to single crochet, with one extra yarn-over at the beg.

A half double crochet st is very similar to the single crochet and double crochet – with a couple of important differences.

Step-by-Step Half Double Crochet for Beginners to make the first half double crochet st.

1. Yarn over (YO) from back to front.

2. Insert the hook into the next st. Put the tip of the hook under both of the loops at the top of the st.

3. Yarn over (YO), and pull the yarn through the st.

You should now have three loops on the hook.

4. Yarn over (YO) the hook again, and pull the yarn through all three loops on the hook.

You should now have one loop remaining on the hook.

Continue across the row.

To make the next HDC: Yarn over (YO) and insert your hook into the next st. Yarn over (YO) and pull through the st. Yarn over (YO) and pull through all three loops on the hook. This completes the second HDC.

Double Crochet(DC)

Double crochet is a taller st than single crochet. It is formed by a "yarn over," which is wrapping yarn from back to front before placing the hook in the st. Holding foundation ch in desired position, yarn over and inset hook into the 4th ch from the hook.

Row 1

1. Yarn over from back to front, and insert the hook into the fourth ch from the hook. (Don't count the loop that's on the hook.)

Note: When you work into ch sts, insert the hook through the center of the "V" of the ch and under the back bar. Be careful not to twist the ch as your work.

2. Yarn over the hook from back to front, and draw the yarn through the center of the ch st. You should have three loops on the hook.

3. Yarn over, and draw the yarn through the first two loops on the hook. You should now have two loops on the hook.

4. Yarn over again, and draw the yarn through the remaining two loops on the hook. The double crochet st is complete. You should have one loop remaining on the hook.

Continue across the row. Make one double crochet st in each of the remaining chain sts in the foundation chain.

At the end of the row, count your double crochet sts. You should have 14 sts: 13 "true" double crochets sts plus the turning chain. (Remember that in double crochet, the turning chain counts as a st.)

Row 2

Now, it's time to make the second row of double crochet. Leave the hook in the work, and turn the piece over so that the backside (wrong side) is facing you.

1. Make three ch sts to bring the yarn up to the correct height for the next row. This ch-3 is called the turning ch.

Remember: Since the turning ch counts as a st, you'll make your first "true" double crochet st into the second st of the previous row.

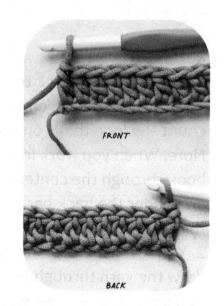

FRONT

BACK

INTO THE
TOP OF THE
TURNING
CHAIN

2. So, sk the first st (the one that's directly below the turning ch), and insert the hook into the next st. Be sure to insert the hook under both top loops of the st.

3. Continue across the row, making one double crochet st in each of the remaining sts.

4. When you reach the end of the row, make the last double crochet in the top ch of the previous row's turning ch. Insert the hook through the center of the "V" and under the back bar.

24

Take a minute to count your sts at the end of the row. You should have 14.
Note: It can be easy to miss the last st! If you're missing a st, go back and double-check.

Finishing Steps

Repeat these steps to make additional rows of double crochet. After the row, cut the yarn, leaving a 6-inch yarn tail. Draw the hook straight up, pulling the yarn tail completely through the st. Pull on the yarn tail to tighten the st, and weave in the ends.

Treble Crochet (tr)

A treble crochet (sometimes called triple crochet) is taller than a double crochet and is made by working two yarn overs at the start of the st, instead of one yarn over as for double crochet. Ready to learn how to treble crochet? Don't worry; it's not that complicated.

Now, let's move on to the step-by-step instructions for making a treble crochet st.

Foundation chain: Start by making a slip knot and ching several sts. To follow along with me, ch 14. This will create the foundation ch into which you'll work your treble crochet sts.

1. Yarn over the hook twice (this means wrapping the yarn around the hook from back to front two times). Your hook should now have three loops on it.

2. Then, sk four chs and insert the hook into the fifth ch from the hook. (The four skped chs count as the first st.)

3. Then, yarn over again and pull up a loop. You should now have four loops on your hook.

4. Yarn over again and pull through two loops. You should now have three loops remaining on your hook.

5. Yarn over the hook twice (this means wrapping the yarn around the hook from back to front two times). Your hook should now have three loops on it.

6. Then, sk four chs and insert the hook into the fifth ch from the hook. (The four skipped chains count as the first st.)

Continue across the first row:

To continue working in treble crochet, rep steps 2-7 in each subsequent st until you reach the end of the row.

When you have worked into the last ch, take a second to count your sts. You should have eleven sts (Remember, the four skped chs at the beg of the row count as a st!)

Magic Ring (Magic Circle)

In crochet, a magic ring is a technique used to start working in the round. It creates a tightly closed center for your crochet project, usually used when starting projects that require working in a circular pattern, such as amigurumi (crocheted stuffed toys) or hats.

A magic circle is a great starting technique to use in crochet projects like granny squares, coasters, potholders, motifs, amigurumi projects or crocheted hats, bags that are worked in the round.

1.Begin by crossing the yarn from the skein (working yarn) over the tail end of the yarn (yarn end) to create a circle.

2. Insert the crochet hook into the circle as shown. Yarn over and pull the yarn from the skein end down through the circle.

3. Step 2 will form a loop on the hook and the circle that you will work into

4. ch 1 with the skein end of the yarn.

5. This step is where you'll start making a single crochet. Insert the hook into circle under both strands of yarn.

6. Yarn over the hook and pull back through the circle of yarn (two loops on hook)

7. Yarn over the hook and pull back through the two loops on the hook. You have now completed your first stitch, a single crochet in a magic circle

8. After you finish your first single crochet st continue by working the remaining sts (the single crochet st used in the example) into the circle by repeating steps 5-7, tighten the ring by pulling the yarn end to close the circle. You have now completed a crochet magic ring!

9. Next, we will learn how to join to make a circle by joining the last st to the first st of the round. Locate the first single crochet you crocheted into the circle. The first ch 1 does not count as a st.

10. Sl sts into the first sc of the round to join the circle to complete the first round.

LITTLE SANTA

Yarn

Scheepjes SOFTFUN
• Fibre content: 60% cotton, 40% acrylic
• Yarn weight: DK
• Length: 140 meter
• Ball weight: 50 gram
• Colours: off-white (skin tone), red, a little bit of black yarn leftovers

You will also need

• 3 mm hook
• 9 mm safety eyes
• polyester fiberfill for stuffing
• tapestry needle
• stitch makers
• scissors

33

Instructions

LEGS

Round 1: Sc 6 in magic ring {6}
Round 2: Inc x 6 {12}
Round 3-4: Sc around {12}
Fasten off. Make the 2 nd leg the same way.

BODY

We will now go on crocheting the body.
Round 5: In this round, we will connect the legs in a circle, ending with 32 sts in total. With the 2nd leg on your hook Ch 4 and connect with the 1st leg with a Sl st. Now Sc around the 1 St leg (12) and work 1 Sc in each ch along the ch 4 (opposite side of the chain). Sc 12 around the second leg and 4 again. Count to make sure you have 32 sts in total.

34

Round 6: (Inc, sc3) x 8 {40}
Round 7-8: Sc around {40}
Round 9: (Inc, sc4) x 8 {48}
Round 10-16: Sc around {48}
Stuff as you go.
Round 17: (Dec, sc6) x 6 {42}
Round 18: Sc around {42}
Round 19: (Dec, sc5) x 6 {36}
Round 20: Sc around {36}
Round 21: (Dec, sc4) x 6 {30}
Round 22: Sc around {30}
Round 23: (Dec, sc3) x 6 {24}
Round 24: Sc around {24}
Stuff firmly. Fasten off, leaving a long tail for sewing.

HEAD

Round 1: Ch 15{15} Crochet in a spiral, on both sides of the chain.
Round 2: From the second chain sc 13, sc 3 in the last chain, turn and continue working on the opposite side of the chain, sc 12, sc 2 in the last st {30}
Round 3: Inc, sc 12, inc 3, sc 12, inc 2 {36}
Round 4: Sc, inc, sc 12, (sc,inc) x 3, sc 12, (sc,inc) x 2 {42}
Round 5: (Sc, inc) x 2, sc 5, inc, sc 6, inc, (sc,inc) x 3, sc 6, inc, sc 7, inc, sc, inc, sc2 {52}
Round 6: (Sc 12, inc) x 4 {56}

Round 7-15: Sc around {56}
Round 16: [Sc 5, dec] x 8 {48}
Round 17-18: Sc around {48}
Round 19: [Sc 4, dec] x 8 {40}
Round 20: Sc around {40}
Round 21:[Sc 3, dec] x 8 {32}
Round 22: Sc around {32}
Round 23: [Sc 2, dec] x 8 {24}
Round 24: [Sc 1, dec] x 8 {16}
Round 25: Dec around {8}
Stuff firmly. Fasten off. Sew the head the body

ARMS

Stuff slightly.

Round 1: Sc 6 in magic ring {6}
Round 2: [Inc, sc1] x 3 {9}
Round 3-10: Sc around {9}
Round 11: [Dec, sc 1] x 3 {6}
Fasten off. Fold in halves and crochet through both layers. Sew arms to the body.

PANTS

Round 1: Ch 60
Connect your chain with a sl st to from a ring. Make sure it fits around the waist. We will continue crocheting in a spiral.

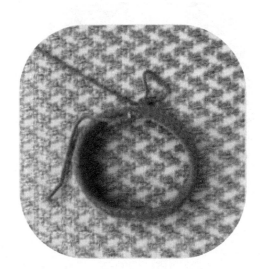

Round 2: Sc 60
Round 3-8: Sc 60 BLO

Round 9: [Dec, sc 8] x 6 {54} BLO
Round 10: [Dec, sc 7] x 6 {48} BLO
Round 11: [Dec, sc 6] x 6 {42} BLO
Fasten off, leaving a very tail for sewing. Place the pants approximately between rounds 15 and 16 of the body, as it is shown on the pictures below.

38

Sew through both layers with the long tail of yarn. Weave in the ends and cut off the excess.

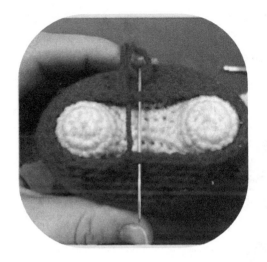 

To make the straps Ch 22. Place them as it is shown on the pictures below. Fasten off, leaving a very long tail for sewing.

BELT

With balck yarn.
Round 1: Ch 60
Connect your chain with a sl st to from a ring. Make sure it fits around the waist. We will continue crocheting in a spiral.

Round 2: Hdc 60
Round 3: Sc 60

Fasten off, waive in ends. You might choose to sew the belt as well.
Now Ch 10 with a yellow yarn to make the buck and sew it to the belt.

HAT

With red yarn.
Round 1: Sc 6 in magic ring {6}
Round 2-3: Sc around {6}
Round 4: Inc x 6 {12}
Round 5-6: Sc around {12}
Round 7: (Inc, sc 1) x 6 {18}
Round 8-9: Sc around {18}
Round 10: (Inc, sc 2) x 6 {24}
Round 11-12: Sc around {24}
Round 13: (Inc, sc 3) x 6 {30}
Round 14-15: Sc around {30}

Round 16: (Inc, sc 4) x 6 {36}
Round 17-18: Sc around {36}
Round 19: (Inc, sc 5) x 6 {42}
Round 20-21: Sc around {42}
Round 22: (Inc, sc 6) x 6 {48}
Round 23-24: Sc around {48}
Round 25: (Inc, sc 7) x 6 {54}
Round 26-27: Sc around {54}
Round 28: (Inc, sc 8) x 6 {60}
Round 29-30: Sc around {60}
Round 31: (Inc, sc 9) x 6 {66}
Round 32: (Ch 2, sc) x 66
Make a pom pom with fluffy yarn.

Decorating the face

1) With black cotton yarn, embroider eyebrows and smile.

2) With the skin-tone yarn, embroider the nose.

CUTE SNOWMAN

Materials

Yarn
Marker
Scissors
Hook

Instructions

LEGS

We make 7ch. from the second loop from the hook we crochet
Round 1) inc, 4 sc, 4 sc in one loop, 4 sc, inc – 16 sc
Round 2) 1 sc, inc, 4 sc, (1sc, inc) *2 times , 4 sc, 1sc, inc – 20 sc
Round 3) 2 sc, inc, 4 sc, (2sc, inc) *2 times , 4 sc, 2sc, inc – 24 sc
Round 4) 3 sc, inc, 4 sc, (3sc, inc) *2 times , 4 sc, 3sc, inc – 28 sc
Round 5-7) 28 sc
Round 8) 10 sc, 4 dec, 10 sc – 24 sc
Round 9) 10 sc, 2 dec, 10 sc – 22 sc
Round 10-11) 22 sc
Round 12) 9 sc, dec, 9sc, dec – 20sc
Round 13) 20 sc
Round 14) 8 sc, dec, 8sc, dec – 18sc
Round 15) Change the yarn to brown. BLO. – 18 sc
Round 16-31) 18 sc

46

We fill in the crocheting process. At the end, fold in half and crochet 9sc on both sides.

Return to row 15 and crochet with white yarn at the front loop – 18 sc

HANDS

In red
Round 1) 6sc in MR
Round 2) 6 inc – 12 sc
Round 3) (1 sc, inc) *6 times – 18 sc
Round 4-7) -18sc
Round 8) 3 dc with a common top in one loop, 17 sc – 18sc
Round 9) (1 sc, dec) *6 times – 12 sc
Round 10) 12 sc
We fill in the crocheting process.
Round 11) Change of yarn to brown, behind the back loop – 12 sc
Round 12-25) 12 sc
Round 26) 10 sc.

Fold the handle in half and watch carefully so that the finger is looking at you. If necessary, + – several sc.

Fold in half and sew on both sides 6 sc.

Return to row 11 and tie with white yarn at the front loop – 12 sc

BODY AND HEAD

We attach a white yarn to the leg, the socks look at you.

Round 1) 9sc for the front loop of the first leg, 9 sc for the front loop of the second leg. Flip, repeat on the other side – 36 sc

Round 2) (5sc, inc) *6 times – 42 sc

Round 3) (6sc, inc) *6 times – 48 sc

Round 4-16) 48sc

Round 17) (6sc, dec) *6 times – 42 sc

Round 18-19) 42sc

Round 20) (5sc, dec) *6 times – 36 sc

Round 21) 36sc
Round 22) crochet 10 sc. We put a marker. The start of the row now starts at this point.
Round 23) 36 sc
Round 24) (4sc, dec) *6 times – 30 sc
Round 25-28) 30 sc
We begin to fill tightly.
Round 29) (3sc, dec) *6 times – 24 sc
Round 30) We crochet the hands. 3sc, 6sc with hand, 6sc, 6sc with hand, 3sc – 24 sc
Round 31) (2sc, dec) *6 –18 sc
Round 32) 18 inc – 36sc
Round 33) (5sc, inc) *6 times – 42 sc
Round 34) (6sc, inc) *6 times – 48 sc
Round 35) (7sc, inc) *6 times – 54 sc
Round 36) (8sc, inc) *6 times – 60 sc
Round 37-50) 60 sc
Round 51) (8sc, dec) *6 times – 54 sc
Round 52) (7sc, dec) *6 times – 48 sc
Round 53) (6sc, dec) *6 times – 42 sc
Round 54) (5sc, dec) *6 times – 36 sc.
Round 55) (4sc, dec) *6 times – 30 sc
We begin to stuff our heads. Do not forget to stuff neck very tightly.
Round 54) (3sc, dec) *6 times – 24 sc
Round 55) (2sc, dec) *6 times – 18 sc
Round 56) (1sc, dec) *6 times – 12 sc
Round 57) 6 dec

Pull the hole, fasten the yarn, cut.
I used a 10mm safety eyes. Placed between rows 44 – 45.

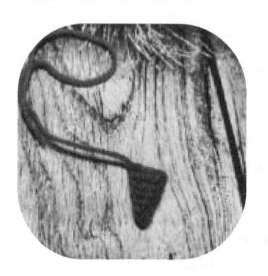

NOSE

Round 1) 4 sc in MR
Round 2) 4 sc
Round 3) 1sc, inc, 1 sc, inc – 6 sc
Round 4) 2 sc, inc, 2 sc, inc – 8 sc
Round 5) 3 sc, inc, 3 sc, inc – 10 sc
Round 6) 10 sc.
We leave the yarn for sewing.

TREE ORNAMENT

Materials

Yarn:
Colour A: Baby Snuggle in Grass
Colour B: Baby Snuggle in Grizzly
Colour C: Gold metallic thread for details
Safety eyes 8mm
Fiber fill
Ribbon
Hook: 5.5mm

Size: 5.5×4.5 in

Instructions

In BLO
Colour A

Row 1: mr, sc 4 (4)
Row 2: (sc,inc)*2 (6)
Row 3: (inc)*6 (12)
Row 4: sc 12 (12)
Row 5: (sc,inc)*6 (18)
Row 6: sc 18 (18)
Row 7: (sc2,inc)*6 (24)
Row 8: sc 24 (24)
Row 9: (sc3,inc)*6 (30)

53

Row 10-13: sc 30 (30)
Row 14: (dec)*15 (15)
Start stuffing
Row 15: (dec)*7, sc1 (8)

1. Complete the tree.

2. Stuff with fiber fill.

3. Place safety eyes between row 9 and 10 of the body with 6 stitches in between.

SMILE AND TRUNK

Colour B

Row 1: mr, sc 8 (8)
Row 2: sc 8 in BLO (8)
Row 3-4: sc 8 (8)
1. Make the trunk. Attach it to the center of the bottom of the tree with fabric. Pins.
Sew on using a darning needle.

2. Using a darning needle and gold thread, make stars through the tree.

1. Place fabric pins where you want the mouth to go on the top and bottom of row 11.

2. Take a darning needle with medium weight black yarn and insert it in the first space.

3. Insert it one row below and push it one row up and one row over.

4. Insert it back into the original spot.

5. Attach ribbon to the top of the tree and tie it.

MITTENS
ORNAMENT

Materials

Yarn:
Colour A: Loops and threads fur in black and white
Colour B: Baby snuggle in dusty rose
Ribbon
Hook: 5.5mm

Size: 4×7 in

Instructions

MITTEN CUFF

Fur yarn
Row 1: slip knot, chain 9, attach 9th chain to the first chain to make a circle and make a slip stitch.
Row 2: sc 9 (9)
Change to colour B
Row 3: sc 9 (9)
Row 4: (sc2,inc)*3 (12)
Row 5: (sc2,inc)*4 (16)
Row 6: (sc3,inc)*4 (20)

1. With the fur yarn, chain 9.

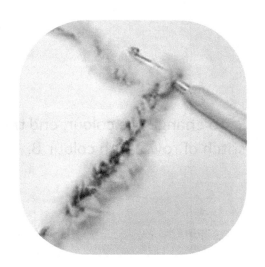

2. Attach 9th chain to the first chain to make a circle and make a slip stitch.

3. To change the colour, end the last stitch of row 2 with colour B.

4. You will want to split the round into the thumb area and the hand area. From the last stitch of row 6, insert hook across so there are 6 stitches on one side and 14 on the other side. Make a sc.

MITTEN THUMB

Colour B
Row 1-3: sc 6 (6)
Gather the last 6 stitches and pull tight.

1. Make 6 sc around for the thumb
piece x3 rounds.

2. Thumb piece complete.

MITTEN HAND

Colour B
Row 1: slip knot, insert into first stitch, sc 14 (14)
Row 2-5: sc 14 (14)
Row 6: (dec)*7 (7)
Gather last 7 stitches and pull tight.

1. Make a slip knot to make the hand portion of the glove.

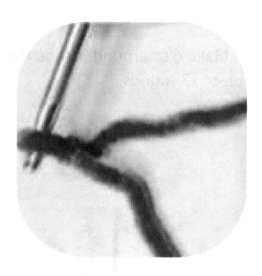

2. Insert into the first stitch after the thumb.

66

3. Continue around to complete the hand portion. There may be a small hole between the thumb and the hand, sew it closed.

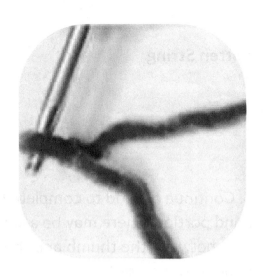

4. Make 2 gloves.

Mitten String

3. Continue around to complete the hand portion. There may be a small hole between the thumb and the hand, sew it closed.

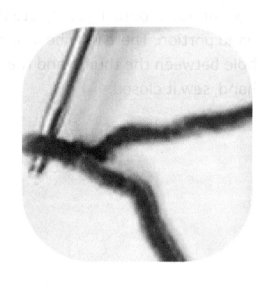

4. Make 2 gloves.

Mitten String

1. Using the fur yarn, make a slip knot.

2. Insert into the outside edge of the rim of the glove where the other fur yarn is. It should be on the opposite side of the thumb. Don't forget to follow lovelycraft.com for 2 new free patterns every day.

69

3. Chain 20 and attach to the other glove with a slip knot.

WATCH ORNAMENT

Materials

Sport weight/4ply yarn Yarn Art Jeans (50g/160m) Of red, yellow, light yellow,
brown, white colors.
Black fine thread
Crochet hook – 1.75 mm or any type you prefer safety eyes 10 mm size
Fiberfill
Beads and rope
Scissors
Needle for embroidery and sewing pieces
Pins for attaching details
Markers

Instructions

WATCH

Start crocheting with brown thread.
Rnd 1: 6 sc in MR
Rnd 2: 6 sc
Change color to light yellow.
Round 3: 6 inc (12)
Round 4: (1sc,inc)*6 (18)

Round 5: 1sc,inc, (2sc,inc)*5, 1sc (24)
Round 6: (3sc,inc)*6 (30)
Round 7: 2sc,inc, (4sc,inc)*5, 2sc (36)
Round 8: (5sc,inc)*6 (42)
Round 9: 3sc,inc, (6sc,inc)*5, 3sc (48)
Round 10: (7sc,inc)*6 (54)
Place safety eyes between rounds 6th and 7th.
Change color to white.
Round 11: 4sc,inc, (8sc,inc)*5, 4sc (60)
Change color to red.
Round 12-18: 60 sc (7 rounds)
Round 19: 4sc,dec, (8sc,dec)*5, 4sc (54)
Round 20: (7sc,dec)*6 (48)
Round 21: 3sc,dec, (6sc,dec)*5, 3sc (42)
Round 22: (5sc,dec)*6 (36)
Round 23: 2sc,dec, (4sc,dec)*5, 2sc (30)
Round 24: (3sc,dec)*6 (24)
Round 25: 1sc,dec, (2sc,dec)*5, 1sc (18)
Round 26: (1sc,dec)*6 (12)
Round 27: 6 dec (6)

Fasten off, sew the hole and hide the yarn tail inside the toy. Embroider the smile and eyebrows with a black fine thread.
Embroider the hands of the clock and dial with a brown thread.

ARMS AND LEGS (MAKE 4)

Start crocheting with red thread.
Round 1: 6 sc in MR
Round 2: 6 inc (12)
Round 3-4: 12 sc (2 rounds)
Fasten off, leaving a long thread for sewing.

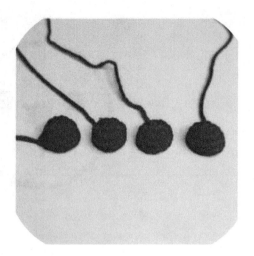

BELLS (MAKE 2)

Start crocheting with yellow thread.
Round 1: 6 sc in MR
Round 2: 6 inc (12)
Round 3: (1sc,inc)*6 (18)
Round 4: (2sc,inc)*6 (24)
Round 5-7: 24 sc (3 rounds)
Fasten off, leaving a long thread for sewing.

ASSEMBLY

Fill in the bells with fiberfill. Sew to the watch. Sew the beads to the bells.

Fill in the arms and the legs with fiberfill. Sew to the watch. Fasten the rope to the top of the watch.

STOCKING ORNAMENT

Materials

Yarn:
Colour A: Baby Snuggle in Brass
Colour B: Baby Snuggle in White
Colour C: Loops and threads fur yarn
Ribbon
Hook: 5.5 mm

Size: 2.5×4 in

Stocking & Heel
5.5 mm hook, bulk yarn

Instructions

SOCK

Colour A
Row 1: mr, sc 6 (6)
Row 2: (inc)*6 (12)
Row 3: (sc,inc)*6 (18)
Row 4-9: sc 18 (18)
Keep yarn on while you complete the heel.

HEEL

Colour B
Row 1: Make a slip knot, insert it 8 stitches from where you ended the last colour. Sc 8, chain 1 and flip.

1. Finish the first 9 rows in colour A. Keep this yarn attached while we make the heel.

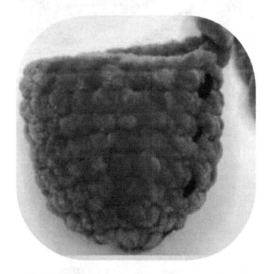

2. Make a slip knot with colour B and insert the hook 8 stitches away from the last stitch of row 9. Make a slip stitch. Make first sc in the same stitch.

3. Make 8 sc across.

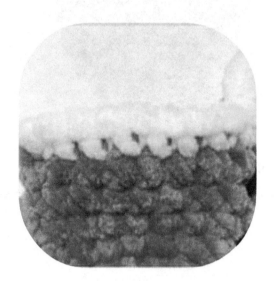

HEEL CONTINUED

Colour B continued
Short Round 2: (dec)*1, sc4, (dec)*1 (6)
Short Round 3: (dec)*1, sc2, (dec)*1 (4)
Short Round 4: (inc)*1, sc2, (inc)*1 (6)
Short Round 5: (inc)*1, sc4, (inc)*1 (8)
Fold in half and sew edges together.

4. Make short rounds by going back and forth, following the pattern.

5. The heel portion should get smaller and then get bigger as in the picture.

6. Once the heel is complete, fold the top part down in half.

84

7. Using a darning needle, sew both edges together. Leave the long bottom edge open.

8. Heel part complete.

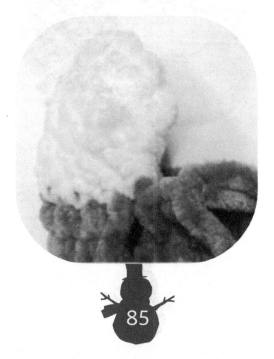

Colour A

After the heel is complete
Row 10-16: sc 18 (18)
Fur yarn
Row 17: sc 18 (18)

1. Go back to the yarn from the end of row 9 that you left on. You will continue around for row 10 that now includes the heel. Ensure you make 8 stitches on the heel portion and 10 sc after that.

2. Row 10 complete.

3. Make the last row using the fur yarn.

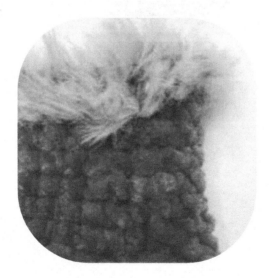

If you notice a small hole from when we did row 10, sew the hole closed with colour A yarn.

Made in the USA
Monee, IL
12 October 2023